WORLD WAR II

JOHN PERRITANO

Created by Q2AMedia

www.q2amedia.com

Text, design & illustrations Copyright © Q2AMedia 2008

Editor Phyllis Baecker
Publishing Director Chester Fisher
Client Service Manager Ravneet Kaur
Art Director Sumit Charles
Senior Designer Joita Das
Project Manager Shekhar Kapur
Art Editor Amit Prashant Tigga
Picture Researcher Kamal Kumar

10 9 8 7 6 5 4 3 2 1

ISBN: 81-905723-2-6

Printed in China

Contents

Introduction

On September 1, 1939, the *The New York Times* announced that the German army had invaded Poland: "GERMAN ARMY ATTACKS POLAND; CITIES BOMBED, PORTS BLOCKADED . . ." the headline read.

For more than a year, the world had teetered on the brink of war as Germany moved unchecked into Austria, Czechoslovakia, Austria, and the Sudetenland. With lightning speed, the German army marched into Poland on September 1, 1939. At the time, no one could fathom that the invasion would be the beginning of the bloodiest war in history. No one could foresee how World War II would change the world for decades to come.

By the time the war ended in 1945, some 72 million people lay dead. The war shattered cities and countries. The war ushered in a new wave of weapons, the most destructive of which was the atomic bomb.

No corner of the globe escaped the horrors of World War II. Although the Axis powers of Germany, Japan, and Italy fought against the Allied nations led by Great Britain, the United States, and the Soviet Union, the war involved countries from every continent.

World War II was the bloodiest conflict in world history. In addition to the millions who died on the field of battle, millions more died in death camps, firebombings, and finally two nuclear blasts that destroyed the Japanese cities of Hiroshima and Nagasaki.

Tyrants and Heroes

While all wars are brutal, World War II was particularly so. The war brought the world some of its most infamous **tyrants** and some of its greatest heroes. In the end, the Allies were victorious. They set up a United Nations to referee disputes between countries in the hope that such conflicts would never occur again.

A new world order also emerged from the war's ashes. The United States shrugged off its cloak of **neutrality** to become the leader of the world's democratic nations. Ironically, the war's end would pit two allies—the United States and Soviet Union—against one another for more than 40 years.

Prelude to War

The Stage Is Set

The seeds of World War II had been planted some 20 years earlier when the First World War ended.

World War I began as a series of political mistakes, fueled by the June 1914 assassination of Archduke Franz Ferdinand, the heir to the Austro-Hungarian throne. Franz Ferdinand's murder, at the hands of Serbian revolutionary Gavrilo Princip, set into motion a series of uncontrollable events that snowballed into conflict.

Europe Torn Apart

World War I—with Germany as its chief **protagonist**—ripped Europe apart. Millions died. Governments fell. Societies collapsed. In 1917, the communists forced Russia's czar from power. Eventually, the great empires of Austria-Hungary, Turkey, and Germany would cease to exist. Riots and strikes in Germany forced the government to surrender.

The "War to End All Wars" ended on November 11, 1918 at 11 A.M. When it was over, more than 40 million people had died. Although France and Britain won the war, the conflict had shattered their economies.

The end of World War I left Europe in tatters. It wouldn't be long before a greater war would engulf the world. ▼

Treaty of Versailles

Diplomats from the victorious nations met in Paris, France, to negotiate a series of treaties with the defeated countries. The Treaty of Versailles was the most important of these treaties.

Seated together in Paris in 1919 are Allied leaders trying to set up a peace treaty after World War I. Left to right: Vittorio Orlando of Italy; Lloyd George of Great Britain; Georges Clemenceau of France; and President Woodrow Wilson of the United States. ▶

Many came to the peace conference with lofty ideals. Some wanted to reduce the number of weapons each country had. Others wanted to allow people to decide for themselves what nation they belonged to.

But revenge, not **idealism**, ruled in Paris. Some nations wanted Germany punished for its role in the war.

To that end, the Treaty of Versailles stripped Germany of its overseas colonies.

The treaty forced 3 million German-speaking people in the Sudetenland to become part of the newly created country of Czechoslovakia. The treaty also severely restricted Germany's military. In a final slap in the face, the Allies required Germany to pay $56 billion in **reparations**—or compensation—for inflicting damage during the war. It was a price the Germans could not afford to pay.

The harsh treaty had laid the groundwork for another greater war. The treaty angered many, including a young corporal in the German army named Adolf Hitler.

The Rise of Fascism

The Great Depression—a worldwide economic collapse that began in 1929 and lasted until the late 1930s—made life hard in many countries. Things were especially brutal in Germany. At the war's end, Germany was broken and tired. There was little to eat and virtually no work.

The Rise of Hitler

The time was right for a revolution. The time was right for Hitler.

Born on April 20, 1889 in Braunau am Inn, a village on the border of Austria and Germany, Hitler dropped out of school when he was 16. He went to Vienna and struggled to make a living as an artist. When World War I broke out, he enlisted in the German army.

Nazi Party

In 1920, Hitler vented his anger against the government and formed the National Socialist German Workers' Party, also known as the Nazi Party. In 1923, Hitler attempted a coup against the government in Munich. The attempt to overthrow the government failed, and Hitler spent nine months in prison.

After he left prison, Hitler rebuilt the Nazi Party. Using violence, fear, and **intimidation**, Hitler and the Nazis won a majority in the Reichstag, the German parliament, in 1932. A year later, with Germany still in dire financial straits, Hitler became chancellor.

When he was a young man, Adolf Hitler struggled to make a living as an artist. After World War I, he formed his own political party. He believed that Germany had been "stabbed in the back" at the Paris peace conference. He blamed the communists, corrupt businessmen, and the Jews for selling out Germany. ▶

Firefighters battle a fire at Berlin's largest synagogue after Nazis set fire to it in an anti-Jewish demonstration throughout Germany on November 9, 1938.

11

Japan on the March

As Hitler and the Nazi Party came to power, the Japanese were on the move in Asia. By 1918, Japan was one of the most modern nations in the Far East. It had transformed itself from an isolated and backward country into an industrial powerhouse.

During the 1920s, Japan's population grew rapidly. Japanese exports were particularly hard hit, and prices fell. Everyone felt the economic squeeze. With little or no natural resources of its own, the island nation had to depend on imports from other countries—particularly the West.

The military and some politicians proposed that Japan force its Far East neighbors into a "Co-Prosperity Sphere," free of Western influence. Within that sphere, Japan would take the raw materials, such as oil, that it needed to survive.

Targeting China

In 1931, Japan's military boldly invaded the northern Chinese province of Manchuria.

The Japanese also began building up its military. In 1937, the Japanese put that vast military to use. A skirmish between patrolling Japanese soldiers and a Chinese unit on the Marco Polo Bridge outside Peking turned into a full invasion of China. The United States and other Western powers condemned Japan's actions, but no one helped the Chinese.

The Japanese invaded Manchuria in 1931. ▶

Hitler's Power

Back in Europe, Hitler had become more brazen. He defiantly ignored the Treaty of Versailles and rebuilt Germany's military. He consolidated his power by eliminating those who opposed his government.

Adolf Hitler defied the Treaty of Versailles and rebuilt the Germany army. He then used that army to occupy other countries. ▶

The Nazis targeted Jews as scapegoats, blaming them for Germany's problems. Hitler preached that Germans were a superior race.

Hitler also grew more aggressive in foreign policy. He and Italian dictator Benito Mussolini signed a treaty known as the Rome-Berlin Axis pact. That pact would later include Japan.

"Peace for Our Time"

Believing Britain and France would let him do whatever he pleased, Hitler grew more daring. In 1938, Hitler ordered troops into Austria and united that country with Germany. Hitler then targeted the Sudetenland in Czechoslovakia, where 3 million German-speaking people lived.

British Prime Minister Neville Chamberlain met with Hitler to avert war. On September 29, 1938, France and Britain told the Czechoslovak government that their countries would allow Germany to send its troops to occupy the area. Chamberlain returned home and declared he had secured "peace for our time." That policy, known as **appeasement**, had preserved the peace for a short while.

Appeasement gave Hitler the opportunity for other territorial conquests. Would France and Britain appease Hitler once again if Germany invaded Poland? The German leader would soon have his answer.

War!

Blitzkrieg

Who was the first casualty of World War II? According to historian Martin Gilbert, it was an unknown criminal. The Gestapo, Hitler's secret police, dressed the prisoner in a Polish army uniform and shot the man on the evening of August 31, 1939. Hitler claimed the Polish army had attacked a radio tower in Gleiwitz.

The next day, German airplanes, tanks, and infantry used the "incident" to sweep into Poland, in a "blitzkrieg," or lightning war. Germany's air force, known as the Luftwaffe, destroyed much of Poland's air force while the planes were still on the ground. Luftwaffe bombers dropped their explosive **ordnance** on roads, communication centers, and bridges. German artillery pounded Polish cities.

A special Nazi force followed as the German army passed through each city, village, and town. The force's job, in the words of Commander Theodor Eicke, was to "incarcerate or annihilate" Germany's enemies.

With lightning speed, the German army moved across Poland on September 1, 1939. The Nazis burned villages and executed Polish peasants and Jews. The invasion was over by October 6. ▼

The Phony War

Before the invasion, Germany had signed a nonaggression pact with the Soviet Union, in which each side agreed not to attack the other. Because of that treaty, the Soviets did not stop Germany's **incursion** into Poland. Instead, the Soviets occupied Eastern Poland. Although Britain and France declared war on Germany on September 3, there was little either country could do to help the Poles.

Poland might have held out a bit longer had the British and French responded. Instead, the British did not have enough troops in the region. Bombing missions launched from Great Britain did little to halt the German advance. For its part, the French army went on the defensive, believing France was Germany's next target. The British and French did not want a bloody repeat of World War I. For several months after Poland fell, not much happened. Europe had settled into a "phony war."

Hitler made a half-hearted attempt at peace, hoping to buy time for his generals to attack Holland, Belgium, and France. In the meantime, the British navy formed a blockade around Germany. British merchantmen tried to keep Great Britain alive by providing the British Isles with supplies. They fended off the German navy and its U boats, or submarines. Back home in Britain, the so-called phony war lulled many people into **complacency**.

During the early days of World War II, German U-boats devastated British shipping, putting a strain on merchant vessels and the British navy. Here, crew members of this German submarine line up for roll call after returning home from enemy waters. This U-boat sunk a British battleship and damaged another. ▶

Dunkirk

The British government sent an **expeditionary** force to try to slow down Germany as the Nazis moved west. As the Germans marched through Europe's lowlands, a new prime minister took over in Britain. Winston Churchill told the nation, "I have nothing to offer but blood, toil, tears, and sweat."

By May 26, the Germans had pushed the British and French into a narrow beachhead near Dunkirk, a seaport in northern France. With their backs to the English Channel and the Germans in front, British and French soldiers seemed doomed. Then ships of every size and shape set sail from Britain and France to rescue the thousands of Allied troops stranded on the beaches at Dunkirk. The evacuation was a success.

Fall of France

With Europe's Low Countries now under Nazi occupation, Paris was in danger. The Nazis began their invasion of France on June 5. Hitler's massive military **juggernaut** rapidly advanced on the City of Lights; and on June 14, German troops marched into Paris.

On June 16, French Prime Minister Paul Reynaud resigned. Deputy Prime Minister Philippe Pétain, a hero of World War I, formed a new government and moved it to Vichy. Pétain called for an immediate truce with Germany. Vichy France and Germany signed the **armistice** agreement on June 22. France had fallen. Great Britain now stood alone against Hitler.

Deputy Prime Minister Philippe
Pétain and Adolf Hitler shake hands
after France surrendered.

The French and British ►
evacuation of Dunkirk was a
success, but it would be years
before Allied soldiers would
once again set foot in France.

The Battle of Britain

"The Battle of France is over . . . the Battle of Britain is about to begin." British Prime Minister Winston Churchill said on June 18, 1940.

On July 2, Hitler ordered his generals to prepare a detailed invasion of Britain. Although Hitler did not set a date for the attack, it was important that the Luftwaffe rule the air before combat troops landed. On July 10, German bombers and fighters attacked a British **convoy** in the English Channel. Another 70 German aircraft bombed the docks in South Wales.

Air attacks soon became a daily fact of British life. During the first 17 days of July, German air raids killed 194 civilians. By August, the battle grew more intense. The Germans launched more than 1,000 aircraft against Great Britain each day. They targeted British airfields and **radar** installations. The skill of British flyers, however, surprised the Germans. By September, Britain took the fight to Germany. By the middle of the month, the Germans had lost 1,880 planes and 2,660 crew members.

The British then launched air raids against Germany's industrial areas, including Berlin. The air raids angered Hitler. He ordered the Luftwaffe to begin bombing British cities— including London.

German bombs destroyed London's Necropolis Railway Station.

St. Paul's Cathedral in London stands shrouded in flame and smoke after the Germans bombed the city. ▼

Londoners camp out for the night in the city's subway system during a bombing raid by the Germans on October 21, 1940.

The United States Helps Out

As Britain bravely held on, the United States decided it had to help. Because the United States was officially neutral, sending troops was not an option. But if Great Britain didn't receive assistance, President Franklin D. Roosevelt feared it would fall.

To help, the United States gave Britain 50 old destroyers in return for British military bases in the British West Indies, Newfoundland, and Bermuda. Roosevelt then asked Congress to pass the Lend-Lease Act. Under the act, the United States provided Great Britain with military supplies in return for payment after the war.

The Russian Front

Great Britain wasn't Hitler's only target. On June 22, 1941, Germany broke its nonaggression pact with the Soviet Union. Some 3 million German soldiers, armed with 4,000 tanks, 7,000 pieces of artillery, and 3,000 aircraft, attacked the Soviet Union along a 2,000-mile-long front. The Luftwaffe destroyed more than 1,000 Soviet airplanes on the first day of the invasion.

Although the Nazi invasion of the Soviet Union at first was quick, the German's march became bogged down by the brutal Russian winter. ▼

A group of German soldiers in a trench during heavy street fighting in Stalingrad.

"We have only to kick in the door, and the whole rotten structure will come crashing down," Hitler said. The Germans code-named the attack "Barbarossa" in honor of Emperor Frederick I Barbarossa, who ruled Germany during the Middle Ages. The Nazis cut through the Soviet Union as they had done in Poland. With lightning speed, the Nazis poured across the border capturing hundreds of thousands of Soviet soldiers.

In August, Hitler made a huge blunder. His original plan had been to push on through to Moscow. Instead, he diverted the German army and encircled 700,000 Russians in the city of Kiev. The delay gave the Soviets time to reinforce Moscow's defenses.

The War Expands

The American Fleet

As Great Britain and the Soviet Union squared off against the Nazis in Europe, and China was left to battle the Japanese alone in the Far East, the United States remained neutral in this ever-widening conflict. President Franklin Roosevelt wanted to help the Allies. However, Congress, and a growing **isolationist** movement in the United States, prevented the government from becoming entangled in another foreign war.

As Europe descended into chaos, things were heating up in the Pacific. By the end of 1941, Western economic sanctions dried up most of Japan's oil supply. The Japanese were determined to survive, even if it meant war with the United States. Admiral Isoroku Yamamoto planned to destroy the U.S. fleet based at Pearl Harbor, Hawaii.

Day of Infamy

The sun rose bright and peaceful over Pearl Harbor on Sunday, December 7, 1941. Just before dawn, six Japanese aircraft carriers had cruised within 200 miles of Hawaii. Their mission was to surprise the Americans at Pearl Harbor and destroy the fleet. The carriers launched 353 planes in two waves of attack.

At 7:55 A.M., the first wave of Japanese planes flew over Pearl Harbor and launched bombs and torpedoes against the U.S. Navy ships anchored close together on "Battleship Row."

The Japanese destroyed or damaged 18 ships during the attack on Pearl Harbor. More than 2,000 Americans died. The battleship Arizona (pictured here) also blew up, killing 1,177 sailors and marines. A day after the attack, the United States declared war on Japan, Germany, and Italy. President Franklin Roosevelt called the attack by the Japanese "a day that will live in infamy." ▶

Mobilizing for War

Almost overnight, America **mobilized** for war. Despite this vast mobilization, the United States was ill prepared for a war. As 1942 began, the time for America to fight had arrived.

The U.S. Army rolls across North Africa in July 1943. ▼

The Soviets, who were battling the Nazis alone in the East, had pressed the United States and Britain to open a second front in Western Europe to take some of the pressure off the Red Army. While the United States favored invading Europe, the British believed such an invasion would be disastrous. Instead, the British wanted to attack Axis forces in French North Africa.

On November 8, 1942, Operation Torch, the invasion of North Africa, began. The Allies planned a three-pronged amphibious landing in Algeria and Morocco. The Vichy French and Allies fought for three hard days.

The Allies forced the Axis troops out of North Africa by May 1943. The Allies could now use North Africa as a stepping-stone to conquer Italy. The tide of the war was beginning to turn.

Expanding an Empire

As American GIs battled in North Africa and swept toward Italy, the battle in the Pacific was raging. The war in the Pacific was chiefly fought in the air and on the ocean with torpedo bombers, submarines, battleships, and aircraft carriers.

After Pearl Harbor, Japan quickly used its massive navy to expand its empire. Guam, New Guinea, the Solomon Islands, and other nations soon fell. The most devastating loss of all, however, was the fall of the Philippines.

Island Hopping

After the Philippines fell, the Japanese continued its conquest of the Pacific. A key island the Japanese wanted was a tiny atoll called Midway, located about 1,000 miles northwest of Hawaii. The Japanese wanted to establish a base there. Admiral Yamamoto, the mastermind behind the attack on Pearl Harbor, wanted to destroy the U.S. defenses on Midway, hoping to draw out and annihilate the American aircraft carriers.

American Marines raise the flag on top of Mount Suribachi on the island of Iwo Jima.

The Americans, however, found out about the Japanese plan and ambushed Yamamoto's fleet. The results were devastating. Japan lost four of its aircraft carriers.

The Americans then devised a simple strategy to bypass Japan's strong points and hit the enemy's weakest links. The goal was to island hop all the way to Japan.

The USS Iowa saw battle many times as the Americans hopped from one island to another. Using this strategy, the Americans won key battles at Iwo Jima and Guadalcanal. Eventually, the Allies reclaimed the Philippines. ▶

The Invasion of Europe

For most of the war, Hitler refused to believe the Allies would invade Western Europe and open a second front. Hitler changed his mind by the end of 1943. In November, he ordered his generals to reinforce all Nazi defenses in the West.

On June 6, 1944, Hitler's worst nightmare came true. The greatest naval armada in history set sail across the English Channel. Thousands of ships and airplanes crossed the channel. The destination: Normandy, France. D-Day, code named Operation Overlord, had begun. Led by General Dwight D. Eisenhower, hundreds of thousands of Allied troops landed at five beaches along the Normandy coast. By nightfall, 155,000 men had stormed ashore.

March to the Rhine

The Allies broke out from the beaches and moved through the French countryside, slowly making their way toward Berlin. As the British and Americans pushed eastward they **liberated** Paris and other cities. The Russians continued to move along an 800-mile-long front from Latvia in the north to Yugoslavia in the south. The Allies were squeezing Hitler and his Third Reich like a vise.

Allied soldiers come ashore in France in 1944. Later that year as the Allies moved through Belgium, the Nazis launched their last counteroffensive, hoping to drive a wedge between the advancing armies. Known as the Battle of the Bulge, the Nazis were unsuccessful. ▼

Canadian troops march through the outskirts of Boulogne, France, in September 1944.

The End

The Evils of War

As the Allies moved on Berlin, they came across some of the most horrific sights the world had ever seen—the Nazi death camps. Nazis had rounded up Jews and other groups and transported them to concentration camps long before the war had started. It was part of Hitler's "Final Solution" to rid Europe of Jewish people.

Jews were rounded up and imprisoned and murdered in concentration camps, such as Bergen-Belsen, Buchenwald, Auschwitz, Treblinka, and Dachau. This systematic, state-sponsored murder of the Jews, became known as the Holocaust. Between 1933 and 1945, the Nazis killed Jews, Roma (gypsies), and the disabled, among others. By the end of the war the Nazis had slaughtered between 9 to 11 million people.

The Big Three Meet

As 1945 dawned, Germany was close to defeat. In February, President Franklin Roosevelt, British Prime Minister Winston Churchill, and Soviet leader Joseph Stalin met in Yalta, on the Crimean peninsula, to decide Germany's fate. At that conference, the "Big Three" called for the unconditional surrender of Germany.

Among other things, the three leaders planned to split Germany into zones of occupation. Each country, as well as France, would control one zone. The Soviets agreed to enter the war against the Japanese. Many historians say the Yalta Conference was the start of the Cold War, an **ideological** conflict between communism and the Western democracies.

◀ *German soldiers surrender to Russian forces in 1944.*

Germany Surrenders

On April 30, with Soviet soldiers advancing on Berlin street-by-street, building-by-building, Hitler committed suicide deep inside the bunker that protected him. On May 7, General Alfred Jodl, whom the Allies would later hang for war crimes, surrendered. The war in Europe was over.

This photo shows the devastation of the first nuclear blast over Hiroshima. ▼

Hiroshima and Beyond

War continued in the Pacific. In early 1945, Allied commanders drew up plans for an invasion of Japan. U.S. commanders feared, however, that hundreds of thousands would perish in the attack. In April, Franklin Roosevelt died, leaving his successor, Harry S. Truman, to make a monumental decision.

Scientists had secretly and successfully tested the world's first atomic bomb. President Truman ordered the military to drop the bomb on Japan, hoping the devastation would bring the Japanese to their knees. On August 6, 1945, a B-29 bomber called the Enola Gay dropped the first bomb on Hiroshima. It exploded above the city in a giant mushroom cloud. Almost 80,000 died instantly. Three days later, the Americans dropped a second atomic bomb on Nagasaki.

On August 15, Emperor Hirohito announced Japan's surrender. World War II was over. A new world order, led by the United States— the world's first superpower—emerged.

Glossary

appeasement—to pacify an aggressor through concessions by sacrificing one's principles

armistice—truce between opponents

complacency—self-satisfaction resulting from unawareness of actual dangers

convoy—group of moving vehicles, such as ships

expeditionary—a military force sent to fight in another country

idealism—the belief that an ideal or perfect situation can be achieved

ideological—relating to a set of ideas or beliefs of a particular individual, group, or culture

incursion—raid or invasion into someone else's territory

intimidation—the act of bullying or frightening others into submission

isolationist—refraining from political or economic relations with other countries

juggernaut—a force that crushes anything in its way

liberated—freed

mobilized—assembled and made ready for war

neutrality—refusal to take part in a war between others

ordnance—armaments, bombs

protagonist—central character

radar—(stands for radio direction and ranging) a device used to locate objects by means of transmitted and reflected high-frequency radio waves

tyrants—oppressors

Sources

Books

Collier, Richard and the Editors of Time-Life Books. *The War in the Desert*. Alexandria, Virginia: Time-Life, 1977.

Gilbert, Martin. *The Second World War A Complete History*. New York: Henry Holt and Company, 1989.

Keegan, John. *The Second World War*. New York: Penguin, 1989.

O'Neill, Richard. *Historical Facts World War II, Turning Points in the Global Conflict That Shaped Our World*. New York: Crescent Books, 1992.

Ross, Stewart. *Causes and Consequences of World War II*. Austin, Texas: Steck Vaughn Company, 1996.

Web sites

"To V-E Day Crowds." *The Churchill Centre*, http://www.winstonchurchill.org/i4a/pages/index.cfm?pageid=428

"The Battle of Britain." *BBC News*, http://news.bbc.co.uk/hi/english/static/in_depth/uk/2000/battle_of_britain/default.stm

Noakes, Jeremy. "The Rise of Adolf Hitler." *BBC History World War II*, http://www.bbc.co.uk/history/worldwars/wwtwo/hitler_01.shtml

United States Holocaust Memorial Museum, http://www.ushmm.org/

Index